Liberated Publishing

Presents…

LiberatedPublishing.com

Liberated Publishing Inc.
1860 Wilma Rudolph Blvd
Clarksville, TN 37040

Copyright © 2014 Adonsia Grant.

All rights reserved. No part of this book may be reproduced in any form or by any means without the prior written consent of the Publisher, excepting brief quotes used in reviews.

The characters and events in this book are fictitious. Any similarities to real persons living or dead are coincidental and not intended by the author.

If you purchased this book without a cover, you should be aware that this book is stolen property. It was reported as "unsold and destroyed" to the Publisher and neither the Author nor the Publisher has received any payment for this "stripped book".

ISBN: 978-0989573238

First Printing: February 2014

Printed in the United States of America

MY HEART OVERFLOWS WITH A BEAUTIFUL THOUGHT! I WILL RECITE A LOVELY POEM TO THE KING, FOR MY TONGUE IS LIKE THE PEN OF A SKILLFUL POET.

PSALM 45:1

DEDICATION

To my Grandma: The matriarch of our family, who holds us all together, who exemplifies love and strength.

To my Mom: Who has been my sounding board, my reality check, my best friend, my support, who exemplifies strength, sacrifice and love.

To my brother: Who is my best friend, who truly gets me and my craziness. A man with a heart of gold, and unmatched compassion.

To my cousins: Who have grown up with me, and to those I have watched grow up, I am truly blessed to have you part of my life.

To my uncles: Collectively ya'll have all embraced me like a daughter, and treated me like a princess. Ya'll have taught me the value of hard work, and truly cared for me as a father would.

To my Aunts: Who have loved me and always provided an example of godliness.

To my running mates: Thanks for catching me when I fall.

To my Grandpa: Although you passed away when I was but a young child, I have taken your memory with me each and every day.

Table of Contents

Confessions of A Wanna Be Poet   9
    Poetic Converse   11
    Writer's Block   12

Confessions Of An Adolescent   13
    Secret Love   15
    Snow For Christmas   16
    Waiting For Christmas   17
    Daddy Dare I?   18
    Separation   19
    Unforgettable   20
    Brutal Words   21
    Brutal Words 2   22
    Trust In Him   23
    America's Flag   24
    10 Steps   25
    Heroes   27

Confessions Of A Woman At War   29
    Battle For My Mind   31
    Life And Death   32
    True Desire   33
    A Scared Evangelist   34
    Creation   35
    Child Of God   36
    A Better Way   37
    God's Love   39
    Chosen   40
    My Heavy Burden   41
    His Voice   42
    Unconditional Love   43
    My Will, Your Will   44

Demon	45
Nonsense	46
Perception Deception	48
Ransom	50
For Your Pleasure	52
In It To Win It	53
Confessions Of A Broken Heart	**55**
Too Bad	57
My Turn	58
Torn Apart	59
Mixed Emotions	60
Even After	61
Confessions of a Celibate Woman	**63**
I'm Sorry	65
And The World Says…	66
The Price of Celibacy	67

CONFESSIONS OF A WANNA BE POET

I confess... when I first started writing poetry I hated it. My first poem was an assignment for 8th grade English class. I didn't know what to write. My first poem was about my grandpa's death, or more about how I felt about it. Of course writing a poem like that in 8th grade English leads the teacher to question your emotional health...so I would choose a happy poem if you have such an assignment in the public school years.

After writing my first poem I found that writing poetry helped me express my emotions. I have been writing ever since that 8th grade English assignment. I have enjoyed writing poetry over the years as it is still proves a good way to express my emotions.

Poetic Converse

Wasn't meant to be spoken
Only meant to be heard
Different form of art
Through the written word
Some people draw
But I paint with the silent tongue
Many have that song stuck in their head
But to me it remains unsung
Poetry is in my voice
Poetry is what I do
May the words flow through me
So they may speak to you.

Writer's Block

On the tip of my tongue
Edge of my brain
Can't think
It'll come soon
These words that I choose
I'm on the brink
People watch me
The pressure is on
Wait for the best
This new page I see
Enticing to me
Put me to the test
Words spill out my brain
Onto the page
Here it comes
New words this page needs
Put challenge to me
Now it's done.

CONFESSIONS OF AN ADOLESCENT

I confess…that after my grandpa died, when I was seven years old, I stopped praying to God. I was mad at God for a long time. Every night I would tell God how mad I was at him for taking my grandpa away and that I wanted to talk to my grandpa, then I would proceed to tell my grandpa everything. When I lost my grandpa I was introduced to fear.

It wasn't until a year or so later that I started talking to God again, and I was no longer mad at Him for taking my grandpa. As I grew a little older, I had a better understanding of death. As I moved from childhood to adolescence I began to let faith overcome my fear.

Secret Love

My secret love
Is the one I see everyday
He'll never know
That I feel this way
With my eye on him
And his eye on her
When I look in his eyes
I know its love or sure
A tap on the face
A pat on the shoulder
If I had one wish
It would be to be bolder
An inch of bravery
Or just to be strong
My love for him
Is it so wrong?

Snow for Christmas

What I want for Christmas
Is not big or small
Short or tall
Dark or light
Dim or bright
No clothes or shoes
No fake tattoos
Not tough or sweet
Nothing good to eat
No perfume
And no vacuum
Nothing I have to tie
Or that says "sold separately"
with pieces I have to buy
I want something I can play in all day and night
Something kind of tall but not quite my height
What I want is nothing you can show
All I want for Christmas is some clean white snow
It should be soft, fluffy, and white
Because it will be ice by tomorrow night
That will make the perfect Christmas day
That is all I have to say.

Waiting for Christmas

Before I looked out my window
Thinking of what I might see
Decorations in houses
And on the trees
There would also be lights
With a wonderful glow
It's no surprise
The ground is already covered with snow
All the street cleaners are cleaning the road
So everyone could get around
Hearing the carolers
Is such a wonderful sound
When I opened my window
There was a surprise to what I did see and hear
Because even when I listened closely
There was no merry Christmas or happy New Year.

Daddy Dare I?

Daddy dare I miss you
When you're a stranger in my eyes?
Could I learn to love you
When you're so full of lies?
Daddy dare I care for you
When you care none for me?
Could I learn to forgive you
For leaving my family?
Daddy dare I keep on going
And survive as I have so far?
Do I really miss a dad
Or do I miss who you are?

Separation

What could never be separated
Was separated after all
The wall that no one thought would crumble
One day did fall
The water that could not be parted
Was parted before anyone knew
The inseparable was separated
And there was nothing we could do.

Unforgettable

I can't believe you left me
Didn't even say goodbye
But I forgive you now
Because you didn't mean to make me cry
You are so far away now
Who knows if we'll meet again
But just for the record
You were my very best friend
But one day our paths may cross
And that secret flame lit
But whatever happens
It is a friendship I'll never forget.

Brutal Words

I hear them whisper
They say my name
Their words do linger
Their talk is vain
Their speech cuts deep
Wounds the soul
Broken to pieces
No longer whole
Their words stay with me
The thought never leaves
But when one pain is ended
Another is conceived.

Brutal Words 2

One word and I'm discouraged
One glance and full of doubt
One critique and question my whole life
And start to wonder what I'm all about
Why your words affect me so much
Or maybe…your lack of confidence in me
Why do I let it bother me so
When I know my capabilities
Your words I will not hear now
No more pity, no more doubt
I will not listen any more
To what you talk about.

Trust In Him

Many people worry
But there's no need to fear
Because he hears your prayers
So don't you worry my dear
He looks after sparrows
And the little birds too
So don't you think that He
Would look after you
So you fell away
And lived a life of sin
Just ask for his forgiveness
And put your trust in him.

America's Flag

You stand for glory
You stand to be free
You stand for our nation
And our country
You've been there with life
You've been there with death
You been there when the enemy
Took our men's last breath
As long as you
Stand for our nation
We'll continue to show you
Our dedication.

10 Steps

10 more steps
Before I never see my class again
Our time is up
Our reign is at its end
9 more steps
Till my moment to shine
I'm stepping out from the crowd
Leaving it all behind
8 more steps
They just called my name
My new life will begin
No more will it be the same
7 more steps
And I'll come here no more
No more early days
No more detention at four
6 more steps
Till no more crowded halls
No more little desks
No more of these same walls
5 more steps
Till no more class clocks
No more dreading that 7am tick
No more anxiously waiting till that 3pm tock
4 more steps
My time is here
No reason to look back
Nothing left to fear
3 more steps
It's time for thanks
The end of senioritis

The end of senior pranks
2 more steps
I'm almost there
Red and blue
The colors I proudly wear
1 more step
I hope I don't trip
Ok I'm ready now
Any last advice? Any final tips?
I'm here
I received my paper, I'm finally through
"Parent's and guest
I present to you, the class of 2002."

Heroes

I never thought you heroes
I never thought you more
I never thought you anything special
Till you ran through that door
I know you saw that fire
I know you saw that smoke
But you ran into the building
To save the common folk
As the world came crashing down
You helped them to the end
Now may you be with God
My dear and trusted friend.

Dedicated to the firefighters and police officers who gave their lives to save others on September 11, 2001

CONFESSIONS OF A WOMAN AT WAR

I confess….that after following God faithfully for three years, in 2006 I considered giving up being a Christian. 2006 was the first time I remember going through spiritual warfare. I was angry every time people mentioned the words God, bible, and church. I got annoyed easily at my friends who genuinely cared about me. Satan purposed to take me out of the race and he fought hard to take my soul.

As I tried to move further away from God and His people, God specifically put one person in my life, who went through the battle with me. No matter how hard I fought her, shut her out, ignored her, and let her know I wasn't interested in her friendship, she loved me. God had already connected us emotionally and spiritually. Soon I realized she was my proverbs 27:17 friend, she was my running mate, and she was my sister in Christ.

Battle For My Mind

his thought
My thought
his will
My deal
he persist
Can't resist
Got to be something better than this
Twenty four seven
Day and night
Never took part in a losing fight
War is done
Battle's not
This is the hardest I've ever fought
Injured bad
About to die
Nothing left to do but cry
So I cry
I NEED HELP
I CAN'T DO THIS BY MYSELF
Cry inside
But no reply
So set the grave
Because here I die.

"For our struggle is not against flesh and blood, but against the rulers, against the powers, against the world forces of this darkness, against the spiritual forces of wickedness in the heavenly places." Ephesians 6:12

Life and Death

Dying is the hardest thing I've ever had to do
So tell me what it truly means for me to die for you
Because I'm lost and confused
Beaten, abused
From this world who claims to love me
But I only feel used
So I quickly turn to you in the midst of my strife
Because you are the only one that will bring life
So now that I am your child you asked me to die
From the beginning I have asked why
"Because your big brother did" that's what you said
"But don't you worry because he didn't stay dead
And just like him I'll raise you up
But you have to understand you must drink from his cup
If you want to know what it means for you to live for me
Look how your brother did in 33 A.D.
Oh my child, I think you really are confused
I want your sinful self to die, for my purpose you shall be used
For you to be used by me, you must turn away from sin
I understand this is hard, but I'll work on you within
Dying is the hardest thing I ever had to see
But you're not called just to die, you're called to live for me."

"I have been crucified with Christ; and it is no longer I who live but Christ lives in me; and the life I now live in the flesh I live by faith in the son of God, who loved me and gave himself up for me." Galatians 2:20

True Desire

My dreams unwanted
Your will divine
Take on yours
Give up mine
Give up self
Do your will
Lay down life
Unspoken deal
One tear loss
One tear pain
All my loss
But bigger gain

"And he was saying to them all, If anyone wishes to come after Me, he must deny himself, and take up his cross daily and follow me. For whoever wishes to save his life will lose it, but whoever loses his life for my sake he is the one who will save it." Luke 9:23-25

A Scared Evangelist

"Make straight the pathway for the Lord!
Get the people ready." He cried
This is really hard to do
I've been out there, I've tried
"Don't be beaten by the past
Go out there and try again"
Ok, but have you seen this world lately
They are consumed and overcome with sin
"That's why I sent you to the lost
To help turn people back to me"
I'm not perfect, my words will fail
I can't speak, don't you see?
"I AM GOD, I AM SOVERIGN!
I have set your mission and decided your call
So go to the lost as I have told you
Trust in me, you won't fall"
Ok God here I go
To start and fulfill this mission
I will trust in you and your word
And on the promise of the great commission.

"And Jesus came up and spoke to them, saying all authority has been given to Me in heaven and on earth. Go therefore and make disciples of all the nations, baptizing them in the name of the Father and of the Son and of the Holy Spirit, teaching them to observe all that I commanded you; and lo I am with you always, even to the end of the age"
Matthew 28:18-20

Creation

You saw my unformed body
A lump of dark, red, clay
When you saw my formation
What words did you say
"Oh my perfect child
You will travel through many lands
But no matter where you go, struggle or succeed
You will never leave my hand
I'll watch over you day and night
And don't worry about being alone
Because I'll always be with you
Until you come back home"

"For You formed my inward parts; You wove me in my mother's womb. I will give thanks to You, for I am fearfully and wonderfully made; Wonderful are your works, and my soul knows it very well. My frame was not hidden from You, When I was made in secret, and skillfully wrought in the depths of the earth; Your eyes have seen my unformed substance; And your book were all written The days that were ordained for me, where as yet there was not one of them. How precious are your thoughts to me, O God! How vast the sum of them! If I should count them, they would outnumber the sand. When I awake, I am still with you." Psalm 139:13-18

Child of God

You told me who I was, as I began to look for you
You showed me who you were, as our relationship grew closer
You said "I will never leave you"
"I am always here" you said
Then why, in so much pain and suffering, I look for you but feel an absence of your presence?
You turned to me and said "I am always here my child. Don't you know that I loved you from the beginning? Can you not feel me when I put my arms around you to comfort you? You are my child, the one I looked or when you were lost. It was I who healed you when you were sick. I LOVE YOU!"
"But you will feel pain and you will suffer. I want to see your faith in all situations, so that I can see Myself in you. So just as my son suffered, so must my daughter. And just as my prince sits with me at my right hand, so one day my princess will sit in my presence."

"In this you greatly rejoice, even though now for a little while, if necessary, you have been distressed by various trials, so that the proof of your faith, being more precious than gold which is perishable, even though tested by fire, may be found to result in praise and glory and honor at the revelation of Jesus Christ."
1 Peter 1:6-7

A Better Way

"I'm scared" I cry
"I'm here" He replies
I don't understand
"Don't worry, let me show you, hold my hand"
"No that's ok" I pull my hand back
"I think I can do it, I'll be ok"
"You sure? Because I can show you a better way."
No, your way is too hard, and I'm too afraid
"Yea, but you want to figure it out right,
That's what you said"
Yea, but I'd rather an easy way out
"That's not the way I work,
Easy is not what I'm about"
Yea I know but there's too much at stake
"That's true, but do you trust me
And the promise I make?
I promise to love you in pain and in health,
I promise to hold on to you
Regardless of the cost to myself,
I promise through this process I'll hold your hand
My child I love you, don't you understand?!"
Ok, Father, where do I start?
"Ok, my child, give me your heart."
OK, can do, what comes next?
"Ok now, I want you to give me your best"
Ok can do, anything else?
"Yes, take down those walls,
 And love them like yourself"
Ok God you are asking too much of me
"No, I don't give you anything outside of your capabilities

And if I do, well that's when I show up"
Ok God, then you must show me who to love,
 Who to trust
"Ok will do, now follow me, be with me,
This is a must"
I would love to, for my heart desires nothing else
To follow you, into the battlefield, forsaking myself
But this whole thing is a journey
And very new to me
So can you lead me, walk with me, carry me please?
"Definitely of course,
I would have no greater pleasure,
For I love you so much!
You are someone that I treasure.
Trust me. I will never leave or forsake you"
Trust you…ok can do.

"Then I said 'Alas, Lord God! Behold I do not know how to speak, because I am a youth.' But the Lord said to me, 'Do not say I am a youth, because everywhere I send you, you shall go, and all that I command you, you shall speak. Do not be afraid of them, for I am with you to deliver you.' Declares the Lord. Then the Lord stretched out His hand and touched my mouth, and the Lord said to me 'Behold I have put My words in your mouth."

Jeremiah 1:6-9

God's Love

You have my soul
You have my heart
There's nothing in this world
That could tear us apart
The enemy tried
But alas he did not succeed
You came to my rescue
And fulfilled my greatest need
I was broken and bruised
When the enemy tried
How I looked for you
But felt alone and just cried
And when I thought I had failed
And could take no more
You came and looked for me
And picked me up off the floor
You took me in your arms
And reminded me of your love
Promised you were with me
Although my trials were tough
Now there's no distance
Nothing separating me from you
Oh how I love you lord
And I know for me, there's nothing you won't do.

"And I pray that you, being rooted and established in love, may have the power, together with all the Lord's holy people, to grasp how wide and long and high and deep is the love of Christ and to know this love that surpasses knowledge – that you may be filled to the measure of all the fullness of God."
Ephesians 3:17-19

Chosen

A bunch of filthy rags I am!
Nothing more, but so much less
I'm not special
Your grace I don't deserve.
A bunch of filthy rags I am!
I don't know much
And I've screwed up a lot
And boy do I have my problems.
A bunch of filthy rags I am!
Not worthy to stand in your presence
Not worthy to hear your voice
Not worthy to see your work…to be your work.
A bunch of filthy rags I am!
Looked on poorly by people
Not thought highly of at all
But you looked at them
…..and you choose me.

"All of us have become like one who is unclean, and all our righteous acts are like filthy rags; we all shrivel up like a leaf, and like the wind our sins sweep us away"
Isaiah 64:6

"What is man that you are mindful of him, and the son of man that you care for him?"
Psalm 8:4

My Heavy Burden

I have the whole world on my shoulder
There's no power in my hand
Oh how will I stand?
God's word comes in a whisper
Satan screams loudly in my ear
Oh I want to hear!
Satan's words overcome me
The loads too much to bear
Do you even care?
I don't know what I'm doing
Or where to go from here
And that's what I fear
You say you're always there, God
Can I really trust in you?
Oh what will I do?

"Cast your cares on the Lord and He will sustain you; he will never let the righteous be shaken."

Psalm 55:22

His Voice

His voice says "I'm a failure,
I can never win,
I may try to do what's right,
But I'm still a slave to sin"
His voice says "no one loves me,
No one really cares,
God left me with this burden,
That's way too big to bear."
His voice says "no one's here to help me,
I'll run this race all alone,
Sooner or later I'll fall back to my old self,
Into the life I've always known."
His voice won't overcome me
With God's help I will stand
I'll defend myself with the shield of faith
And with the sword in my hand.

"Therefore if anyone is in Christ he is a new creation. The old has passed away; behold, the new has come."

2 Corinthians 5:17

Unconditional Love

Do you still love me father?
Although I disobeyed
I have heard all your commands
But did not follow a word you said
Do you still love me father?
Although I've turned my back on you
And although I try to do what's right
I still did what you didn't want me to
Do you still love me father?
Even though I try to hide
Instead of confessing my sins, I looked at you…lied and justified
Oh how can you love me father?
Your unconditional love, I hope soon to understand
As I look to obey your will
And not follow the ways of man.

"But God demonstrates His own love for us in this: While we were still sinners, Christ died for us."

Romans 5:8

My Will, Your Will

How can I bring you glory,
Oh, I long to do your will
And how I want to trust you
But I can't just sit still
My feet follows my desires
My hands long for control
What's the risk of not choosing your will
I believe, what's at stake, is my soul.

"Many are the plans in a person's heart, but it is the Lord's purpose that prevails."

Proverbs 19:21

Demon

Dark face
Red eyes
Move fast
No disguise
What's your purpose
"GO AWAY!
BEHIND ME SATAN!"
This I say
Attack my will
Attack my might
At first sight
Another fight
With God's help
You can't stand
Evil stomped
By his holy hand
Another battle
We just won
Another victory
War's not done.

"And unclean spirits when they saw Him, fell down before Him, and cried, saying, You are the son of God"

Mark 3:11

Nonsense

I know what's right
I know what's wrong
I live this life
My morals gone
I live in sin
What to do
I'm so lost
I look to you
What's nonsense?
Life of course
Live intense
And live with force
Or sell out
Hang head in shame
Live in doubt
Who's to blame?

All my readers listen up, this is what's up, we must learn how to follow Christ and drink from his cup.

This poem is about a girl who knew what was good, what was hidden from others, she understood.

She knew her Lord's plan, and her father's desire. His word burned in her so, she was on fire.

To share his love with the world, that was the plan. But she fell in love with the world, so she could not stand.

Now she looks for him she cannot find, it's hard to look at sin when you're the divine.

She will come back when she learns how to give, give her life for others, give her life to him.

But right now she has fallen away, and right now here she will stay.

How she strayed so far when she knew what was right, when she was good and precious in sight.

It's me who I write about and I write it intense, how I live my life right now, no excuse…just nonsense

"I do not understand what I do. For what I want to do I do not do, but what I hate I do. And if I do what I do not want to do, I agree the law is good. As it is, it is no longer I myself who do it, but it is sin living in me. For I know that good itself does not dwell in me, that is, in my sinful nature. For I have the desire to do what is good, but I cannot carry it out. For I do not do the good I want to do, but the evil I do not want to do – this I keep on doing. Now if I do not want to do, it is no longer I who do it, but it is the sin living in me that does it."

Romans 7:15-20

Perception Deception

Living in a whole new world
Feeling like a whole new girl
Come so far from where I use to be
Look at myself in the mirror and I admit, this isn't me
What happened to me
And the girl I used to be
All the changes
I'm now famous
I look back on my past
See that my strength didn't last
I need help
I need to look outside myself
To not go back
Accepting no slack
But moving forward
Toward
The goals I use to have
No going back to the past
This new me won't last
Become someone better smarter
Working harder
To get where I need to be
Where I can start to recognize me
One day I'll get there
And I'll just stare
Because I'll be who I need to be
Look like what I need to see
Let all of me free
From the captivity
Striving for a whole new goal, so I can be a better me.

" This is what the Lord says- he who made a way through the sea, a path through the mighty waters, who drew out the chariots and horses, the army and reinforcements together, and they lay there, never to rise again, extinguished, snuffed out lie a wick : 'Forget the former things; do not dwell on the past. See I am doing a new thing! Now it springs up; do you not perceive it? I am making a way in the wilderness, and streams in the wasteland'."

Isaiah 43:16-19

Ransom

I'm not frightened
I'm not afraid
But I didn't know
He wanted a ransom to be paid
I thought he liked me
But I didn't see the chains on my hands
He finally came to me
And made one demand
"I want your life"
Ok, I thought it was easy enough to give
However, my king stepped out in front of me
And asked me to live
I started to see freedom
Then looked down at my chains
"I can give you that freedom
Your life, and hope" the king claimed
"But she is my hostage!
She has turned to me!"
"Ok give me her sentence
Her punishment, and penalty"
"Ok I demand death
Death on a cross"
I know He's the King
But how can he pay this cost
A king's life for a peasant
"No, a princess" He replied
He paid my ransom
So I don't have to die
No more chains on my hands
Now I am free
I once was blind

But now I see
OH NOW I AM FREE!

"Then you will know the truth and the truth will set you free. They answered him 'We are Abraham's descendants and have never been slaves of anyone. How can you say that we shall be set free?' Jesus replied 'Very truly I say to you, everyone who sins is a slave to sin. Now a slave has no permanent place in the family, but a son belongs to it forever. So if the son sets you free, you will be free indeed'."

John 8:32-36

For Your Pleasure

Here on earth for your pleasure
Excited to do your will
But caught up in confusion
What's the deal?
Am I doing this thing right?
I'm consumed with self-doubt
I'm trying to live this life right
Longing to know you, seeking you out
So what are your standards?
How can I know when you are pleased?
Is it when you see the fruit,
Or when we plant the seeds?
I guess I'll keep on doing what
I know you like to see
And even though I mess up some
Please be pleased with me.

"...and whatever we ask we receive from him, because we keep his commandments and do the things that are pleasing in his sight."

1 John 3:22

In It To Win It

I hate this world
And most of what's in it
I hate this world
But I'm in it to win it
When I want to give up
And I'm ready to cry
He reminds me of my purpose
And tells me "multiply"
I hate this world
And most of what's in it
I hate this world
And the prince that's in it
I fight him on this battle field
That has no grass or trees
When the King comes to claim his land
He'll bring satan to his knees
"Come and learn my plan
Cause time is near its end
And I'll show you how to reconcile
The world to me again
I'll show you how to love them
With the love I've shown to you
Hate the sin and not the man
And you will love them too"

"Dear friends, since God so loved us we also ought to love one another."

1 John 4:11

CONFESSIONS OF A BROKEN HEART

I confess…That I fell in love with a man that lied to me, cheated on me, never really loved me, and had a baby with a woman I worked with while we were together. Yet, I loved him so much I still wanted to be with him.

AT the age of 29 I have only been in three relationships in my life, but only one have I truly loved. I became everything this man needed me to be, to include a mother figure to his son. I loved more than I knew I could, I wept more than I ever had, and the pain I felt, I believed to be unbearable. Through the pain and the tears God brought me to a place of pure desire. I desired God more than I ever had before. He brought me to a place of dependency, surrender, and contentment. Although I suffered more than I thought I could bear, I do not regret being put in that situation. For it was through this situation that God pulled me so close to himself that I fell in love again, but this time with my maker.

Too Bad

He didn't know how much I loved him
Or how much I cared
Or how much I truly treasured
All the times we shared
Too bad I never told
How much he meant to me
That I wish our love was forever
Now all that's left…is the memories
Too bad.

My Turn

I took my turn for pain
I took my turn for sorrow
I took my turn for heartbreak
Will my turn for joy come tomorrow?
I took my turn for loneliness
I took my turn for tears
I took my turn for emptiness
Will my turn for true love come this year?
My turn will come when I am still
And God's will I do
My turn will come when I let go
And surrender it all to you.

Torn Apart

I'm scared to love
Because I'm scared of pain
If I let people in
I might get hurt again
So now I fear relationships
And fear that no one cares
A place where my heart once was
A hole now resides there
When you left you took my heart
I have nothing more to give
Oh that life would keep us apart
Saying you should die and I should live
Will I learn to love again
And who would take my heart
Because it's beaten and bruised, and slightly used
And still remains torn apart.

Mixed Emotions

I cry because you do not care
When I could've swore you did
I curse because you make me mad
With every word you said
I fear because I love you so
When I get none in return
I'm sad because you left me here
When my heart with passion burns
I cry because you said you'd call
So I waited day and night
I curse because you piss me off
And all we do is fight
I fear because I might lose you
And that is not what I need
I'm sad because no matter what I say
I know you want to leave.

Even After

Even after you cheated and the child came to be
Even after you showed me you did not care about me
Even after you told me you had no love for me
I loved you
You might always retain a spot in my heart
But there is no room for you in my life.

CONFESSIONS OF A CELIBATE WOMAN

I confess…that I was celibate for 23 years of my life. At the age of 23 that changed, and I compromised my convictions. It was the worst thing I felt that I have ever done in my life. It became a foothold for the devil to use against me for many years. I couldn't bring myself to face God, so I turned my back on him.

It took a few years but I soon forgave myself, and once again God rescued me from satan's grip. I no longer look at myself through what I have done in the past, but I view myself through the blood of Christ. I have been made a new creation and no longer stand condemned even though satan would try to have me believe it. I now stand on purpose and conviction, I do not move far from my Savior's reach. I am celibate and have been for years, and I am not ashamed. I walk a different path than the rest of the world. My path is narrow and my friends are few. This path may lead me to a life of singleness and being childless. However, I will not turn from it, I will not consider no other path than the one that leads straight to my savior. My eyes are focused, my feet are set, my path is marked, my will is strong, and my God is in control.

I'm Sorry

I'm sorry I didn't wait or you
But it's funny because I prayed or you
I told myself that God would see me through
But when it came down to it, I lost faith in you
And in God, cause I didn't believe
I betrayed you, as would a true daughter of Eve
I thought giving in would make me relieved
But as I stand in your presence
 I find it hard to breathe
And as I stand in His presence I fall to my face
Because as He looks at me,
 I know I bring Him disgrace
And as I run away from Him he continues to chase…me
And I know if I let Him He will choose to embrace…me
But I refuse to be loved so I continue to run
I rejected the father and so reject His son
He said He'd fight for me and that the battle is won
And that all I have to do is turn to the One
The one who has the power to forgive
Who would give me strength to live
That I would no longer be a captive
To the sin that was so active…in me
So now I turn back to you
My head, my lover, my future husband, my boo
I ask for your forgiveness too
For not being able to wait for you.

And The World Says…

You're waiting for what?
You're waiting for who?
Naw girl I'm straight
I want nothing to do with you
Come on how about this one time?
I know you want it right?
Oh…you going to keep on waiting,
Ok, you going to be single your whole life
You think your future husband is waiting for you,
And you trying to save yourself for him?
You passing up on something great
Because you keep on saying it's a sin.
Fine…keep your virtues,
Keep your conviction
Keep your virginity
While I go enjoy this sin.

The Price Of Celibacy

I'm not saying I'm perfect
But I'm pretty darn close
I've treated you better than your ex
Matter of fact I've treated you better than most
I've treated you like a king
Sitting upon his throne
I cooked, I cleaned,
A hot meal ready when you came home
You have a son, that's no problem
I can be a mother too
Help with homework, feed him, clean him
Anything for you
I did nothing but better you
Push you toward your full potential that is
Then you had the nerve to tell me
You slept with "that" and had another kid
Are you serious right now?
I thought our relationship was nice
I guess you're just one more reminder
That celibacy has its price.

Adonsia Grant, poet and author of *Confessions,* grew up in the small town of Clarksville, Tennessee. Her travels, adventures, and personal experiences have provided influence for the poetry she writes. She has performed at poetry readings and speaking events over the past ten years. She now pursues a bachelor's degree in business management, as well as a degree in early childhood education. She hopes that she can relate with people through her poetry, and share the joy she has in Christ with the world.

Liberated Publishing Inc
1860 Wilma Rudolph Blvd
Clarksville, TN 37040
info@liberatedpublishing.com
931-378-0500

www.LiberatedPublishing.com

www.ingramcontent.com/pod-product-compliance
Lightning Source LLC
Chambersburg PA
CBHW071635040426
42452CB00009B/1635